Advanced Praise for

AIN'T NO
SHAME

*It is refreshing to read something so realistic that
I relate to, but just don't talk about. I think the
author is a strong person who is able to persevere,
especially during difficult circumstances.*

  *This book encouraged me. I am young and
still learning about myself and how to deal with
shame, trauma, and anxiety. Reading this book
made me realize that I'm not alone—everyone has
similar experiences. When she discussed family
"secrets," that was helpful, too.*

~Aiyanna Harrell

***

*I recommend this book to anyone who has ever
experienced trauma. It will help you understand
trauma and that you are not alone.*

~Sharon Hartzog, MA, LSW,
LCSW, LCSA-A

***

This book is for those who think they are lost and can't find their way.

~Minister Mary Mitchell,
Deaconess and Teacher

AIN'T NO
SHAME

AIN'T NO
SHAME

Embrace The Past,
Accept The Present, and
Move On To The Future

TREISHA PARKER COMBO

DEDICATION

To the strong women in my life who have passed on: **Grandma Mamie, Aunt Gloria, Grandma Shirlene,** and **Aunt Ruth:** they were unable to overcome their shame, but we are still here and we will come out of it.

FOREWORD

Before I met Treisha Parker Combo, I met her mother, Mrs. Mary Parker. I was working as a personal care assistant at Victory of Faith Home Health in Cofield, North Carolina, and Mrs. Parker worked in the office. Throughout our relationship, Mrs. Parker has become a blessing to my life. As a mother-figure would do, she supported me in the idea of making extra money and encouraged me to become a business woman. That's when she introduced me to her daughter, Treisha. We hit it off instantly and became great friends. After meeting her, I joined her in two businesses: selling jewelry and helping people with their financial health.

I lead a Bible study with a group of women and when I invited Treisha to join us she was enthusiastic. For years she has been a faithful participant, offering a listening ear without judgment, and praying for others in good times and bad times. Treisha is led by her faith in God and her testimony is authentic and raw. This is why I believe *Ain't No Shame* is valuable reading.

In the Black community we talk about how we don't go to therapy. In this book, Treisha reminds us that it's okay to go to therapy and speak with a trusted therapist because it allows a person to talk out how shame is effecting them and their family.

I thank God for my relationship with Treisha. Even though I didn't know it at the time we met, she departs wisdom into me and it strengthens my faith. She has done her best in teaching me the ropes with building relationships and sales, now she is sharing some of this wisdom with you. Open your heart and receive not only Treisha's testimony but allow God to heal places that you hide in shame.

Aminitta Holloman, President
~Women of Worship (W.O.W.)

ACKNOWLEDGEMENTS

To my handsome husband **Tremaine**—
Thank you for always being there for me.

To my **Parents**—Thank you for loving me
and teaching me how to be strong and
independent.

Tonya and **Tori, my sisters**—I appreciate
ya'll so much for your support in all of my
endeavors.

Nyasiah, **Takyia**, and **Ninah**, my
children—Y'all have given me purpose and
for that I am truly grateful.

To my church family—**Victory of Praise
Ministries**, and my pastor **Magalene Powell**,
for all the prayers and encouragement along
the way.

Thank you **Shiwana Rucker**, for your
keen eye for edits.

Thank you to my wonderful Scribe Coach
Penda L. James— I thank God for you. He
has a way of always putting things together,
I really appreciate you for being such a big
help in this process.

Contents

A TAURUS IS BORN

"I am a Taurus.
The bull is strong."

~Treisha Parker Combo

I came into this world in 1977, in the quaint town of Ahoskie, nestled within the beauty of North Carolina. My childhood in Ahoskie was marked by the presence of wonderful people who shaped my life.

The essence of the town was characterized by several key elements: the close-knit community, the sense of belonging fostered by our local church, the bonds of family and friends that held us together, and the comforting embrace of the small-town ambiance. If you aren't familiar, Ahoskie is 40 minutes from Suffolk, Virginia and 45 minutes from Rocky Mount, North Carolina.

My daddy is a quiet man. I don't know how he pulled Ma, but whatever he said to her at the Tastee Freeze in Woodland, North Carolina must have worked. She was 15 and he was 17 when they became a couple and they got married in December of 1971 in

Emporia, Virginia. My parents have been together for over fifty years. Now that I think about it, there are many threads of commonality in my family. For example, my mother and her mother both had children when they were sixteen years old. Ma dropped out of high school in the tenth grade. Tragically, at 18 months old my brother Mark was taken from us due to a devastating accident. Sadly, the details surrounding Mark's passing have been shrouded in silence within our family.

I recently came to understand the heart-wrenching events that unfolded that day. As a woman in her forties, I am awed by the incredible resilience of my mother after learning these details.

My parents were blessed with four children. Alongside me are my older sister Tonya, and my younger sister Tori. We grew up right off of Highway 561 in an area of Aulander, North Carolina called "St. John." Ironically, some of my hometown friends call us "561 Chics," which is a nod to the street where we grew up.

When my sisters and I were grown and out of the house, Ma expressed her desire to get her General Education Diploma (GED). We all supported her, and she passed the test. Watching Ma press on without allowing any of her life experiences to prevent her from accomplishing her dreams and goals inspires me. My upbringing has made me tenacious and passionate as a wife, mother, and daughter. I have modeled my strength after her.

My parents have taught me many lessons. I loved cutting the grass with Daddy. I was like his shadow. Where he went, I went. I saw how hard they worked every day for everything that we had in the seventies and eighties. Growing up, I never observed anything unusual in my family.

Ma shared with me how they had to make ends meet sometimes. There were moments when debt was high and it was necessary to borrow money to keep us afloat. I remember seeing Ma use green stamps from a grocery store to buy food. I didn't know back then that using those green stamps meant we were living paycheck to paycheck. I knew we were not rich, but we were living good in my eyes.

Family Ties

Family was everything to us. I was always around kin because we have a large, extended family between Ahoskie and Aulander. My daddy's daddy, Joe Lee Parker had an employer who sold him an acre of land. As a family we always had a safe place to go.

One of our neighbors, Ms. Mae Roni Harrell used to get on my last nerve. She was an older lady who lived alone in a house. I don't know how she saw everything from across the street, but whatever we were doing, good or bad, she reported it back to my parents. As an adult, I can appreciate Ms. Mae Roni; she was a great neighbor who took being part of our community seriously. She did a good job of looking out for us.

I wasn't close to Ms. Mae Roni, but I had a strong connection with a few people in my family at an early age. My father's Grandmother, "Grandma Mamie" is one of those people. In her later years, Grandma Mamie lived with my cousin next door to us. I would go over to their house every day. In the mornings I went before getting on the school bus and in the evenings we would watch television and talk until she got ready for bed.

I looked forward to my time with Grandma Mamie; that's probably why I like hanging out with older people now. Back then I couldn't believe that she gave birth to seven babies. Her husband, Gus, had five children by his first wife. She raised a lot of children.

My paternal grandparents had nine children. At one point Aunt Ruth and her two children lived with us in our three-bedroom trailer. Although we had two bathrooms, only one was usually fully functioning. My sisters and I shared one room, my aunt and her family shared a room, and Momma and Daddy had their private room.

I don't remember our house being noisy, but there was always someone around. I looked forward to escaping to Grandma Mamie's when I wanted some peace and a few minutes of quiet time. Sitting with her at the kitchen table when she drank her coffee calmed my soul.

. . .a friend loves at all times.

~Proverbs 17:17

AIN'T NO
SHAME

I LOST MY BEST FRIEND

A major life moment happened to me on November 9, 1984. I was in the third grade, and that morning, I headed over to Grandma Mamie's house before I got on the bus. I tried to walk the stairs up to the porch, but my cousin Jean and my mom didn't let me step inside of the house.

Ma said, "Get on the bus and go to school." I obeyed her and turned around. I don't remember walking to the bus stop, nor do I have any real memories of what happened at school that day. Everything is a blur from the time she told me to go to school. They didn't tell me that Grandma Mamie had died that night, and I couldn't go inside because the undertakers had not yet come to get her body.

I have been trying for most of my adult life to process the grief of losing someone I loved so deeply at such an early age. I recall that Grandma Mamie's funeral service was on a Saturday, but my sisters and I weren't allowed to go. I didn't understand at seven years old how not getting to say goodbye to Grandma Mamie would stick with me even into my forties.

I wish my parents had asked me if I wanted to go to the funeral. I think they were trying to shield me from my grief, and I understand that position as a parent. As a child, being unable to say goodbye to Grandma Mamie complicated the grief I was already feeling. Thankfully, someone gave me some pictures of my family at her repass to remember that day.

After Grandma Mamie died, I reached a point in my young life when I stopped caring about anything important to me. My unprocessed grief manifested itself in a lackadaisical approach to my schoolwork. I was proud of my academic success and in third grade, I was thriving; I even earned an award for reading 75 books at school.

That next school year, I was carrying so much heaviness from losing Grandma Mamie that I didn't have the energy for school when I started at R.L. Vann for fourth grade. I had trouble taking tests, and they moved me down to intermediate reading.

My teachers didn't try to understand what had shifted. Ma didn't know what to do. She listened to the teachers and did what they told her to do. The school put me into the special education program. My most vivid memory of that time was having to go to lunch with children who wore helmets. That was no fun.

Something in me fought hard to get back to where I was supposed to be educationally. By the end of the year, I was on target for fifth grade and back on track scholastically. Ironically, my parents don't even recall my time in those special education classes. Daddy thought I was in classes for smart students.

*The fear of the Lord is
the beginning of wisdom;
all who follow his precepts
have good understanding.*

~Psalm 111:10

AIN'T NO
SHAME

THE CURIOUS YEARS

At the age of nine I got my first job working in the tobacco fields. It was during the summer of 1986 and I was trying to be a big girl like Tonya who was trying to make extra money to buy clothes. It was the only job I could get at the age of nine. Ma felt safe with me being out there with Tonya and some of her friends.

Farm work is not easy, let me tell you. It was hot out there and I didn't have a good hat to protect my skin from the sun. I called myself "High Yellow" back then because I was so light and I got a bad sunburn. I'm not playing; that stuff hurts!

I was scared of the snakes out there. Whenever someone cut their heads off with a hoe, I got squeamish. I had a hoe, and I remember walking down the rows, but I couldn't do too much because I didn't have the same strength to swing the hoe as the adults. That job made it clear that I did not want to work in a field for the rest of my life. My tobacco field days only lasted a week; I collected my $60.00 check and I was done! I went back to being a kid, watching television and enjoying my lazy summer days.

The Change

Later that year, I started my menstrual cycle. At the time, I was in the bathroom and I yelled for Tonya, "I got blood in my underwear!" She threw some pads in the bathroom and said, "Put one on." I knew how to put a pad on because I learned from friends, but I never had a conversation with my mom or dad about what cycles meant, sex, or what was happening to me.

That summer, I went swimming at Water Country USA in Williamsburg, Virginia. I put on a tampon, but no one told me how to insert it. I left the plastic applicator on; you can probably imagine what happened in the pool.

I started sixth grade when Murfreesboro, Ahoskie, and Winton schools combined to form Hertford County Middle and High Schools. My friends and I were the first class to attend the combined school.

HIGH SCHOOL

*"High school is about finding who you are, because
that's more important than
trying to be someone else."*

~Nick Jonas

I prepared for my freshman year at Hertford
County High School in the fall of 1991. That
summer, I learned a lot of lessons from Tonya
that kept me out of trouble. She was working
at Burger King and hanging out with her
friends. I watched as she enjoyed her
newfound independence since she had
graduated that spring, but she clashed with
Ma at times.

I remember one time she got in trouble and
Ma beat her up and down the hall. I felt so bad
for Tonya, I started crying. Ma looked at me
and said, "What you cryin' for?"

I had tried out for the cheerleading squad
before school started, but I got cut. When
school started, I joined the Drama Club and
participated in talent shows with some of the
561 Chicks. I worked hard and kept my grades
up while staying out of trouble.

Freshman year was a lot of fun, but I had some heartache too. I fell in love with a light-skinned Indian boy. I used to skip school with him, wasting my time trying to be around him. I let him go when I found out that he was cheating on me; that broke my heart. I put my head back in my books and started hanging out with my friend Daniel who kept me focused.

In my sophomore year, I gained more confidence. I met Addrain on a school field trip with the Drama Club. He was nice to me and tried to talk to me on the trip but I blew him off. On the bus ride home we sat together and talked all the way home. I took his fitted cap and wore it backward. We kissed for the first time, and we started dating.

Addrain would drive me home from school. Keep in mind that I was 16 and the light-skinned boy and I had just broken up! Thinking about it now, I probably should have taken a break from dating. But who has time for that?

I started Junior year with enthusiasm. In my second semester I had a Finance class. Most people thought Mr. Charles Freeman's class was boring, but I was intrigued by what he taught. Mr. Freeman was a short white man who wore glasses. He was one of my favorite teachers.

Taking Mr. Freeman's class was pivotal for me. A light bulb turned on, illuminating the possibilities of what my life could become. My family didn't have much, but Mr. Freeman helped me believe that I could acquire and accomplish many things. If I followed his blueprint and implemented what he taught us about money, I knew I'd be okay. By the time I was 17, I had purchased my first CD for $1,500. I earned $300 in 18 months.

In Mr. Freeman's class, I learned about the value of saving money, the purpose of investing, and how to buy a Certificate of Deposit (CD). Mr. Freeman helped us apply for and interview for jobs to apply what we learned in his class. I was excited because I had seen Tonya and her friends working at Burger King. They seemed to enjoy themselves with the money they made.

I was 16 when I was hired as a cashier at the main store in our town, the Piggly Wiggly, in 1994. That job was a big difference from the tobacco field! I loved it because I got to help others and see people that I didn't normally get to see. Around food stamp time some of the customers could become aggravating and impatient. That didn't bother me. I still smiled and gave them my best customer service.

When I first started my job, I didn't have a car, so my momma had to drop me off and pick me up. Once I got into the groove of working they spent $1,000 to buy me a car like they did for Tonya.

I found a car, bought it, and kept up the maintenance on it, but that car kept giving me trouble and it eventually died. I found a five-speed 1989 white Pontiac Grand Am. I didn't know how to drive a manual speed, so I ended up slamming into the back of somebody on my way to Suffolk, Virginia, to buy my prom dress. I put the car in the shop and when I got it back, it turned out looking better than it did before.

My manager's name was Jerry. He must have seen something decent in me because he thought enough of me to ask if I wanted to work in the office. I was still in high school, and the office ladies, Ms. Mary, and Ms. Jane, were all mothers enjoying their lives with their kids. When they got off of work I would take over the office. My job was to generate the Western Union money transactions and money orders. I felt accomplished doing that job, because Mr. Freeman's class gave me the confidence to do my job and do it well.

I stayed at Piggly Wiggly until 1997 and saved as much money as I could.

Senior Year

I don't have a lot of memories from my last year of high school because I was working and going to school. Even with that, I couldn't figure out what I wanted to do after I graduated. I thought about becoming a lawyer but I figured out how much schooling I would need, which was a deterrent. Then, I could not lie with a straight face and as a lawyer I would have to do whatever it took for my client, so that changed my mind about law school.

In Health class, listening to my teacher, Ms. Cooper, who was a registered nurse, talk about her career inspired me to want to become a nurse. She acted like nursing was so glamorous. Because Ma had earned her Certified Nursing Assistant (CNA) I already knew that I wanted to go into the medical field. I had a lot of family members who were CNAs so I already had decided to pursue that track.

Ma had helped her cousin Carolyn Mosely and one of her friends start a home healthcare business. My passion for nursing was developed as I watched her help others accomplish their dreams. When I was much younger she worked for rich white families and in the summertime, we would get to go to their houses. Seeing all of their big farms and the fancy things inspired me.

A few years later Carolyn opened up her own home healthcare business with Ma's help. Carolyn has passed, but the business is still operating as of today. For most of my life,

I have seen the benefits of being a small business owner, which has always been one of my aspirations.

Two of my friends talked about going to nursing school with me, but I was the only one who went. One went to Elizabeth City State University to study Social Work, and the other went into medical assisting.

I went to the prom with Addrain wearing a hunter-green velvet dress with a slit up the side. It looked so much better on me than the purple dress I picked for Junior Prom. Ms. Barbara, a family friend, put finger waves in my hair. I will never do that again, but otherwise prom was fun.

By the time I was ready to graduate from high school in 1995, I had decided that I was going to apply for the nursing program at East Carolina University (ECU), which was my dream school. I quickly realized that admission into the nursing program was not easy. Only 25 people were admitted a year. I have had trouble taking tests since fourth grade. I didn't do well on my college entrance exams. I think I got a score of a 420, and they give you 200 for writing your name.
I didn't let that stop me; it did slow my progress a little.

*...let the wise listen
and add to their learning,
and let the discerning
get guidance.*

Proverbs 1:5

AIN'T NO
SHAME

ON TO NURSING SCHOOL

My parents didn't have $40,000 per year set aside for me to pay for college. I attended Roanoke-Chowan Community College (RCCC) in Ahoskie. I was excited that I was attending college even though I was staying with my parents. When I got the scores for my entrance exam I had to take a few extra classes because my reading score was low. I worked at Piggly Wiggly and paid for the CNA program, and within two months, I graduated.

After I got my CNA, my goal was still to become a Registered Nurse and I slowly worked at it. One night while watching television with my dad, we saw a commercial for Medical Career Institute (MCI) and he said, "Hey, do you want to go there?"

I called MCI the next day and scheduled an appointment to visit the school. Daddy took a day off of work from the shipyard, and we went to Newport News, Virginia, to check it out. I took the admissions test, completed the application, and was accepted that day. The counselor was able to help me get financial aid in the form of loans, and I started school two months later.

I didn't mind commuting to school. I had a reliable car, and sometimes I would drive from Ahoskie to Como, North Carolina to carpool with my friend, Freda. One time, we were riding home from class and got caught in traffic on the James River Bridge. Freda and I were at a standstill in traffic when an older lady in a beat-up Dodge van hit her Jeep Cherokee. She said she rammed us in the back because she didn't see us.

I felt fine after the accident and didn't go to the hospital from the scene. When I tried to get out of bed the next day, I couldn't move. It was very hard to turn my head. I cried out, "Mama, come help me!"

Ma took me to the hospital, and the doctors diagnosed me with whiplash. I had to go to physical therapy for discomfort, neck, and head pain. The doctor explained that it would take some time, to feel better. It took a lot of work, but I finally got back into alignment. From that experience, I now believe it is important to keep my body in alignment.

Freda called an attorney and advised me to reach out to someone. I found an attorney who negotiated a financial settlement for me. I was awarded a sum of money, and I used some of it to start a mutual fund and some to pay off the student loans for LPN school.

Moving Out

The drive to school started taking a toll on me after the accident. When my grades started to slip, I decided it was best for me to move closer to school. I was 19 and thought I was grown. Addrain decided to move to Newport News with me. We found a one-bedroom apartment for $425 a month, and to pay the security deposit I cashed in the CD that Mr. Freeman had helped me purchase.

In February of 1997, my parents and I loaded my daddy's F-150 with all of my things. We waited for Addrain, but he was late. My daddy does not play. When it was time to go Addrain got left! He had to drive to the new apartment on his own.

I picked up the keys to my apartment and we unloaded the truck right before Addrain arrived. We locked up the apartment and hit the thrift store to buy some furniture. We bought a set of mattresses, a sectional, and a kitchenette. My television took up most of the wall in that small apartment.

I was going to nursing school full-time and working part-time at Food Lion. Addrain was taking care of his expenses, and I got another job as a CNA at the hospital to cover the bills. I must say I did well in nursing school while working two jobs.

Getting Married

Addrain asked me to marry him, but I wasn't ready to get married. I was content living at home with Ma and Daddy. I wasn't thinking about marriage at the time. I was enjoying my youth.

When casually talking to one of my classmates in school, she asked me about my relationship status. "Are you married?" she asked.

"No, I said, "but I'm dating someone."

She said, "If something happens to him, you have no say so in what happens. You won't be able to make any decisions because you are just the girlfriend." She was from Mississippi and she was an old soul in her thinking. She was married, so I believed her.

I went home that night and said to Addrain, "We gettin' married." I had eleven months left in nursing school.

On April 26, 1997, a few days before I turned 20, I married my high school sweetheart in my parent's front yard. Everybody was there—people from church, neighbors and family. Tori did my hair for the wedding, and Tonya was my Maid of Honor. Ms. Carol, my neighbor, baked my cake, and Ma and my aunt's cooked the food. It was a good day. Unfortunately, we couldn't take a honeymoon because I had to get back to school.

Not long after the wedding, Addrain and I started looking for a house; I really wanted to get out of our tiny apartment. I found Ms. Dot, a real estate agent, to help me. She started talking to me about life insurance and securities.

I was making good money as a CNA and decided to get life insurance for myself and my new husband. Ms. Dot introduced me to Jeff Watkins, her Regional Vice President in Primerica. I was open to learning more about money, mainly because Mr. Freeman had laid a good foundation for me in school.

He talked me through purchasing the insurance policy, and I was inspired by his support and knowledge. Because I had used my CD to pay our apartment's security deposit, I knew it would be beneficial to start saving money again. Jeff helped me start a mutual fund. Eventually, he started teaching me how to talk to people about life insurance and wills.

I finished the 15-month LPN diploma at MCI on March 13, 1998. I took the test five times, but finally, in August of 1999, when I was 22, I passed. As soon as I earned my nursing license I went to work at Riverside Hospital.

If I could go back and encourage my 21-year-old self I would tell her, "I know that life for you has been a little hard. Just know that it will all be worth it." At that age, I was working so much and I couldn't imagine how much better my life would be as a 46-year-old woman. I didn't see myself being able to travel the way I do or having some of the luxuries that I have now.

As I sit here thinking about myself at that age, I wouldn't change a thing that has happened to me. Life is good. I've grown and learned so many things. I would tell myself, "Treisha, keep smiling. You are stronger than you think you are. You have greatness within you; let her out."

BECOMING A MOTHER

"I love being a mother."

~Treisha Parker Combo

Addrain and I had a difficult time getting pregnant. We tried all kinds of procedures, but I couldn't conceive for some reason. We did three rounds of invitro fertilization, and none of them worked. I was getting tired and frustrated, and when I finally stopped those treatments I got pregnant.

On the morning of December 19, 2002, I had a regularly scheduled prenatal appointment. Usually, the nurses would check my blood pressure, weigh me, and make me go to the bathroom to check my protein levels. When she checked my blood pressure it was high that day. For several appointments it had been out of control.

I had to sit in the room for 30 minutes to see if it would decrease. When the nurse came back and checked it, my blood pressure was still high. I was a nurse and knew the symptoms of preeclampsia, but I hadn't experienced any. My doctor was on vacation, and his physician's assistant came into my room and said, "Ms. Bishop, we can't get your blood pressure down. We need you to go to the hospital." I didn't realize I was sick and I thought everything was good. Being sent to the hospital as a 25-year-old first-time mother, I was scared sh-tless.

I cried as I drove from the doctor's office to the hospital in the next lot. I thought to myself, "My child is not ready; she has three more weeks to bake." I wasn't ready either. I was expecting her on January 8, 2003.

Addrain and I had taken pregnancy photos the night before to commemorate the birth of our daughter. I put on a burgundy cotton top that accented my belly. I laughed because I was fat as hell, yet excited. It had been a long journey for us trying to get pregnant, and it was finally happening.

We had just moved into our new house and boxes were left unpacked. I had just had my baby shower, and the house was not ready for the baby. Nothing was done. Her crib wasn't put up, and nothing was put in the drawers or closet. In that moment, while driving to the hospital, I realized things were happening too fast for me.

My baby was coming, whether I was ready or not.

Before I checked into the hospital, I called my job, crying. The receptionist was my friend, and I explained that I was on the schedule but couldn't make it to work. I was never one to miss work. She was comforting and she said, "I will let everybody know, and we will be praying for you."

I called Addrain at work. I called my mom and one of my aunts. My aunt tried to be helpful and told me to take St. John's Wart. I asked the nurse about it, and she informed me that it was not recommended for people in my condition.

I was in the hospital, laying on my left side, and I sent Addrain to get me fish sandwiches with extra tartar sauce and fries while they tried to get my baby to come on her own. My parents were at the hospital waiting for her arrival. After four days of no progress, I had to have a C-section.

I asked my sisters about what they remember from December 23, 2002. My sister Tori said, "Nothing came to mind; it was a long time ago." She nor my sister Tonya were there when the baby came, but Tonya gave me an account of what she remembers:

> *I was not there until after everything had happened. We were told that you said you did not feel well a while after giving birth. The doctor came in and dismissed you not*

feeling well, stating it was normal after giving birth.

They said you coded, and the doctor did CPR for about 45 minutes to an hour. The next time we saw you, they had put you on a breathing machine and in a medically induced coma. They told us it was to help you heal.

I cannot remember how long you were on the breathing machine, but I remember one time you woke up and tried to pull out the tube in your mouth, and they put you back out. They said all we could do was wait for the end result.

We waited and prayed. It was the same time the pregnant Peterson woman went missing. She did not make it home, but to God be the Glory, you did.

Emotions were high, and it seemed like a lot was going on."

The hospital staff told my family everything was fine, and they all went home to get some rest. Around 1:00 a.m., I started having trouble breathing. According to my medical records, I abruptly developed respiratory distress, tachypnea, and hypoxemia. Basically, I was having difficulty breathing. The X-rays showed that I had Cardiomegaly (enlarged heart) and pulmonary edema. The doctors sent me to the nuclear medicine department to see if they could identify blockages in my heart.

I developed Orthopnea followed by Cardiac Arrest while in the nuclear medicine department. I developed Congestive Heart Failure (CHF) and, Prolapsed Mitral Valve.

The doctors restarted my heart, and I was put into an induced coma to allow my body time to heal. As this was happening I could see myself and I could feel the presence of my Aunt Gloria.

I did have an out-of-body experience, and I stood at the gate of heaven, but I could not go in. I remember looking down at my body. I distinctly remember that my Aunt Gloria was right there with me. Whenever she touched me, I would feel revived. She touched my head, and there was a transfer of energy given to me.

I have no other memories of anything that was happening around me during that time, but I know that the Lord was protecting and shielding me from death. I stayed in the ICU for about a week. Addrain brought Takyia to see me when I was in a coma.

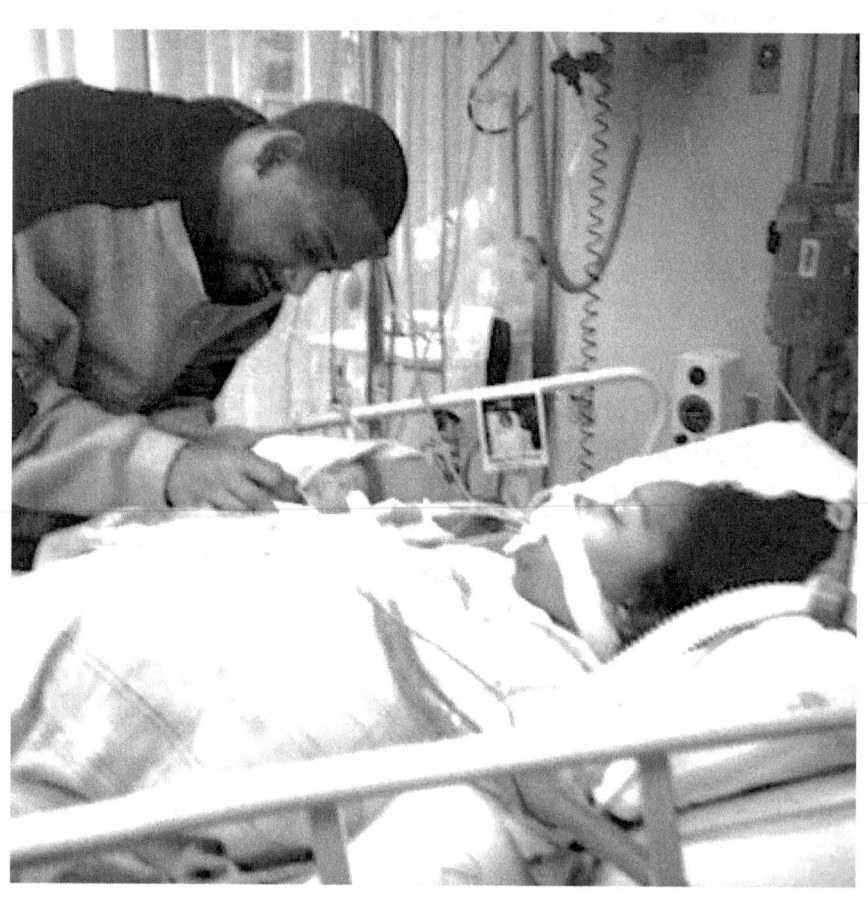

HEALING AND RECOVERY

Jesus went throughout Galilee, teaching in their synagogues, proclaiming the good news of the kingdom, and healing every disease and sickness among the people.

~Matthew 4:23

It has been two decades since I received the diagnosis of Congestive Heart Failure (CHF), and during this time, I have been leading a comfortable life supported by Disability. While I have harbored a deep desire for healing, I often hesitated to bring this to God in my prayers.

Whenever the idea crossed my mind, I would dismiss it with self-doubt, telling myself, "Treisha, things are good. Why disrupt the stability you have? You have everything you could ask for, from a place to call your own to a reliable monthly income." Little did I realize that this internal dialogue was a tactic employed by the enemy. Yes, my circumstances seemed fine, but I was neglecting the very mission that God had entrusted me with.

I'd reassure myself, "You're consistently paying your bills, and your financial standing is great. You've mastered the art of budgeting and managing your money wisely. So, why do you complain? God has been looking after you and your family."

While I believed I was content, my complacency was hindering the divine purpose set out for me. I have been granted the responsibility to assist others and be of service. My volunteer involvement in a nonprofit organization and my multifaceted roles within the church allow me to educate people on financial matters. I have always had a strong aspiration to aid people in any way possible. I enjoy helping others.

At my church, one of the pastors used to always ask the congregation, "What do you want from God?" That question stumped me. I knew then that I had to get my life in order and my first step was to pray more. I wrote out Scriptures and read my bible three times a day. I asked God to show me His way, and He answered me with a book called *God's Creative Power for Healing*. I do not remember when my momma gave it to me, but I started to read it and it helped me to visualize myself getting better.

The author, Charles Capps wrote, "Your words are building blocks of which you construct your life and future." He talks about how God has given us everything we need to be healed and free. We have to pay attention to our words and what we speak over ourselves. Capps wrote, "Your faith frames your world daily." He emphasizes how everything around us plays a part in the things that are happening in our lives.

Since being diagnosed with CHF, I have had to get myself back in alignment with God. For over 20 years, I needed to take heart and blood pressure medication. Recently, I was able to have my heart medication reduced and I take blood pressure medication as needed.

I desire to be healed. I know that God could have healed me anytime He wanted to. I believe He was waiting for me to ask Him to heal me.

Some people can find that one little thing that keeps holding them down. No matter how great things are going for them, they can find a reason not to rejoice. I have embraced Mr. Capps' teaching and started to pray for healing. When I turned my heart to God and asked for healing, I lost 29 pounds, and began to get my life back on track.

When I am around negative people or listen to negative things, it affects me. When I was intentional about my healing, I had to limit the time that I spent with certain people because of the lifestyle that they were living. I had to stop watching certain TV shows that did not line up with my values. We mirror what we see and hear. I am going to get real deep with y'all for a moment. I am a TV watcher. At times I watch too much damn TV. For real, I do. I have enjoyed Tyler Perry's works since he came out with his first plays and movies. I was good until I saw one of his shows that started with a couple in a barn having sex. His shows were not the only ones I had to stop watching. Olivia Pope was one of my favorite characters, but I had to stop watching *Scandal.* Even *Days of Our Lives* was a little too much for my mind to handle.

I thank God for the Holy Spirit, who guides me because there have been times when I have seen things on television and had dreams about it. That is one of the reasons that I do not watch a lot of scary movies. Yeah, you can call me a "punk" all you want. It's okay. I have a hard enough time trying to stay focused on my own life, I do not need other things in my head from crazy television shows and movies.

Because of what the book by Charles Capps taught me, my pastor's teachings and my faith, I can envision myself in excellent health. I feel good and I can envision the life that I was supposed to have. My medical condition caused me to lose sight of my dreams, but I am focused on achieving everything God has designed for me.

BROKE AS HELL

Addrain and I had many differences in how we approached paying our expenses, and eventually, our marriage ended. In 2004, I filed for divorce. It was hard as hell being in a relationship with someone who did not value my money the same way I do. Plus, I was a tither. I always put God's money first.

By November 2005, I was a single woman. I was a stay-at-home mom, which I grew to love, but once she got old enough I put her in daycare so that she could get used to being around other children.

After Takyia was born, I could no longer work my full-time job. I remember crying on my bed when I called my job to tell them I couldn't return. That was hard for me, and I felt ashamed.

I applied for WIC when she was five months old, and when I was approved, it was a win for us. Baby formula and milk were not cheap, especially because I was on a tight budget. Addrain did help with expenses from time to time, and I was able to stay on WIC until she turned five years old.

That was the first time I had ever needed any type of assistance. Having to ask for help felt like a hard punch in the stomach. It was all new to me and on top of it, I had never lived on my own before and we had just moved into a new house.

I was paying a mortgage and a car payment with no job. The only money coming into my house was short-term disability from my job. Things were really tight. I tried Social Services and guess what? I was making too much money and they could not help me.

Ironically, as a 27-year-old woman I was out in the clubs trying to catch up on all the stuff I had missed out on living the "traditional life." Newly divorced, I was enjoying going out to clubs and having fun. My wing girl was always ready to go out with me. We loved ladies night when the male strippers were performing. I made a few male friends along the way and they used to slide me their numbers and ask me to host private parties for them.

I was the only one of my friends who owned a house so I hosted private parties for my friends. At times there were up to 40 people who paid $10 at the door to get in. I used that money to help pay bills.

The parties could get really live. One night, they set up a blue plastic pool in the middle of my living room. One of my friends had a friend who sold lingerie and adult toys. Let me tell you, everything that looks good in the club, is not always what it seems. After a few yeast infections I learned a hard lesson.

Over time, some of my so-called friends and I had to part ways, which was for the best. I was out of control and needed to get my sh-t together. I was setting a bad example for my daughter. Plus, when I needed help paying my bills, I knew I could not ask my parents to cover for me. I knew I was wasting my money going to the club. I did not want them to know I was going to the pawn shop up the street from my house to pawn jewelry for new clubbing clothes. (Don't tell anyone).

The short-term disability was not enough to cover all of the bills. My church family helped, and it was nothing but God's grace and mercy keeping me. I felt depressed. I felt that I had built a life that was supposed to be perfect, but it was falling apart. I had to grieve the person I once was and find the new me.

And my God
will meet all your needs
according to the riches of His
glory in Christ Jesus.

~Philippians 4:19

AIN'T NO
SHAME

Good Friends

Thankfully, I had good friends who helped me along the way. One of my middle school friends gave me a blessing. During one phone conversation, he noticed that I was coughing, and he said, "Is that the same cough you had three weeks ago?"

"Nah, I'm alright," I said. I really had not thought about how long I was coughing. I said, "I ain't got no money to go to the doctor right now." My Medicare had not kicked in yet, and I was still on Cobra insurance from my previous job. The cost to visit the doctor would have been money out of pocket that I did not have.

The next day, my friend's Mom showed up at my door. She handed me some money in an envelope and told me my friend had sent her. I was thankful he cared that much for me, and wanted to help me out, yet I was also ashamed that I was barely getting by.

Eventually I went back to school to earn my Nursing degree and graduated in 2007. In 2008, Takyia and I moved to North Carolina to be closer to my sisters because I needed to be around my family. Although I missed my old friends, I would go back to visit often.

A MOTHER'S LOVE

Her children arise and call her blessed.

~Proverbs 31:28

I do not know if Takyia will ever understand the kind of sacrifices that I have made for her, or my other children. I do not mind putting my children's needs before my own. I am their mother.

Making Sacrifices

I used to shop at the thrift store for myself but would pay full price for Takyia's clothes. One year, I was in Las Vegas on vacation, and I was on Facetime with her, shopping for school clothes. I had to buy another bag to ship things back home.

Making sacrifices for my child, I learned how to make plans and dreams big for myself. I always believed I would live on my terms when my children got old enough. As soon as Takyia graduated from high school, I would live life to the fullest, enjoying every moment dancing, listening to music, and traveling to places like Hawaii, Paris, and Jamaica. I planned to take care of myself while singing and making people laugh. I was saying, "Okkkur. I'm done," in my Cardi B. voice.

Sacrificing for Takyia, I always knew I was going to have to increase my self-care. When she graduated from high school, one of the first things I did for myself was see an orthodontist and get braces. Our dental insurance did not cover orthodontics for me when she had braces. My smile is important to me. It took me a while to realize my own beauty, but I see me. And I love me more than ever.

When she was little, Takyia sucked her two middle fingers. It was hard to get her to stop. I tried hot sauce, pepper, anything I could think of, and nothing worked. Takyia's finger-sucking caused her teeth to push forward. By the time she was six, she needed braces badly. Thankfully, her dad had dental insurance to cover the cost of the monthly orthodontic appointments. It was no fun for me, because on every visit, I had a copay. Takyia had three sets of braces that lasted over six years. During that time, we moved from Virginia to North Carolina. I continued to take her to the same orthodontist in Virginia and had to drive three hours once a month for adjustments.

Co-pays. Gas. Mileage.

I did not care about the money I was spending; I wanted my baby to be healthy. When Takyia was young, she had difficulty sitting "crisscross applesauce." She never crawled. She just stood up and started walking on her tiptoes. Doctors thought that she had Cerebral Palsy. I drove Takyia all over Virginia to different specialists, trying to get results and answers.

The last place I took her was Children's Hospital of the King's Daughters (CHKD), one of the best pediatric hospitals in Virginia. They could not figure out what was wrong, either. All they said was that she had an "unsteady gait."

Takyia wore special shoes and braces for her legs, but nothing helped her. The doctor visits and the prescribed methods of rehabilitation were not cheap. She had to have physical therapy three times a week, and the co-pay was $50 per visit.

It felt like I was wasting money and my baby was not getting better. We moved from Virginia to North Carolina, and I got her into physical therapy again. One of the therapists sent us to Duke Hospital. After reviewing her x-rays, he knew exactly what the problem was.

Takyia had surgery, and she would not have been able to do that if I had not found the right doctor for her. God is good!

FINDING LOVE, AGAIN

He who finds a wife finds what is good and receives favor from the Lord.

~Proverbs 18:22

In 2005, I gained powerful insight from TD Jakes' series, "The Lady, Her Lover, and Her Lord." I borrowed this VHS video series from my mother. It featured several different ministers. One sermon lingered in my mind because the preacher talked about how past intimate connections could potentially leave a spiritual imprint on us. The preacher broke down how as you lay with other people, spirits can transfer between people. I knew that the Lord could not dwell in that. This notion stuck with me, and during that time, I was motivated to get myself together.

I was involved with someone who had relocated to Florida to attend school. I had a dream that I surprised him with a visit only to find out he had moved on without me. I kept trying to reconnect with him, but it proved futile. It became evident that for me to progress, I had to let go of him. Taking this dream and the sermon to heart, I initiated a change.

I decided to abstain from dating and intimate relationships. For four years I was focused on my personal and spiritual growth. Eventually, divine intervention played its part, and Tremaine entered my life at church where he was assisting his mother with her catering business. Oddly enough, I had seen him in a dream prior to our first encounter, but all I could recall was his attire; Tremaine's face remained elusive.

In 2007, three years before our marriage, out of the blue, Tremaine called me while I was at my mother's house. He was living in Elizabeth City, North Carolina, but was visiting his mother in Cofield, 15 minutes from my mom's house in St. John. He came to pick me up and we spent hours driving around and talking. I knew I still needed to work on myself before entertaining a serious relationship.

Life's challenges persisted as I sought alignment with my faith and personal development, unbeknownst to me, these experiences shaped me for my future husband. For years, I studied the Bible to become the wife that God intended me to be. My go-to scriptures were Proverbs 31, Mark 10:9, and Proverbs 18:22. God wants wives to be full of wisdom, honor, and strength. A good wife respects her husband, and is kind, intelligent, and patient. I studied my word and stayed in church to become these things.

While working on myself, I enjoyed traveling and trying new things. In 2009 my sisters and I went on a cruise to Mexico and Key West. We had a good time on the cruise. The thought was far from my mind about getting into a relationship or dating. I was focused on having fun and spending time with my sisters. We made some great memories, one of them is when we crossed paths with Al Roker filming a show. I felt like a movie star.

I love taking pictures. This is one of my favorites from that trip.

Upon my return from the cruise, I discovered a message from Tremaine on my answering machine, providing his contact details. I knew Tremaine and his mom because she caters a lot of events at my church. In August of 2009, Tremaine and I started talking exclusively. Our interactions flourished, including letter-writing and Skyping while he was deployed in Iraq.

A Marriage Proposal

In October 2009, Tremaine proposed, offering a budget for my engagement ring. With my sister Tonya, we embarked on a ring shopping adventure while Tremaine guided us via Skype.

After he proposed, I found myself meeting with Tremaine's parents alone. My nerves were real, and I did not know what to expect. It was a lot to navigate meeting his dad for the first time and his mother as her son's fiancée. I visited them one Sunday after church. Their curiosity led to a barrage of strong questions as they tried to protect Tremaine, their oldest son. He is more than five years younger than me, and their first child to get married. Thankfully, I navigated the situation and survived the questioning.

I returned to his mother's house to spend the day with them on Christmas and to have a family Skype call with Tremaine. I was sitting downstairs while his parents talked with Tremaine upstairs. Nyasiah and Ninah, his daughters from a previous relationship, approached me and asked if they could refer to me as "Mama." With a smile, I accepted without hesitation. Takyia said she was okay with it. Being part of a blended family was new to Tremaine and me, but we made it work.

In February of 2010, upon his return from duty, Tremaine proposed to me again on Valentine's Day at Shoops Landing in Winton, North Carolina. His brother, Terrence, accompanied us, taking memorable pictures.

On March 12, 2010, we exchanged vows at his parents' house. We had a honeymoon weekend at the Turtle Cay Resort in Virginia Beach, followed by a week in the Poconos, gifted by his parents. The scenic drive to the Poconos proved worth it, especially when it unexpectedly snowed during our stay. Dressing up for dinner remains a vivid memory, etched in my mind as if it happened yesterday.

Blending Our Families

I want my children to be successful. I do not want to enable them, and even though it is difficult for me, I have to let them fall and fight to get up the way my parents taught me.

All my girls have graduated from high school, and all three are in college. We talk or message daily. As they got older, social media took over and we did not talk as much. I learned I had to meet them where they were, in a texting world. I always tell them that I love them and I express my pride about them. I encourage my girls, and I question them, too. And if there is a time when they need me they call or text me. I still talk to my mom and dad daily. Sometimes I even ask them for advice because I am constantly learning; no one knows everything.

Every chance that I get, I talk to my children about life and their future. I remind them that they can do anything they put their minds to. I tell them, "There is no limit to the things that you can accomplish. If you want it, work hard and go get it."

If I ever told my children that they are worthless, or that they will never become successful, that is probably what would have become their reality. To prevent your children from living in shame, keep the lines of communication open, speak positively to them, and pray for them daily. Your children are not you. You have to allow them a little space to mess up and make mistakes. That's how they learn. I do not speak badly to my children and expect them to give me their best. That will never work.

Love and Marriage

It has been over 13 years and we can push each other's buttons, but Tremaine and I make an awesome team. Please do not get it twisted; we have good days and bad days, but we love and respect each other. Through the years, we have been really, really blessed. As a wife, I submit to my husband because I want to recognize God's authority.

Tremaine and I pray together and I pray for every aspect of his life. It was initially a battle for me because I was so independent, but now if we have a disagreement, I pray and let God fix it.

Love and marriage take work. We have built our marriage with the Word of God as our foundation. I believe that marriage is a triangle. God is at the peak; my husband and I are on the sides. As we draw closer to God, we draw closer to each other.

I thank God for the lessons I learned from my previous marriage, and I will not make the same mistakes. I promised myself and God that I would not bring the shame from my past mistakes into my new marriage.

DREAMING BIG

In 2017, my husband was dreaming big about buying another house. He wants a huge house so our girls and their future families can stay with us during the holidays. I liked his vision, but thought, "The house we live in is comfortable enough to host everyone." When Tremaine shared this dream with me, I had to get on board to help make it happen for us.

Tremaine was going to be deployed overseas, and I needed something to do to keep myself busy so that I did not worry about him too much. I invested in myself and spent around $110.00 to join Paparazzi Jewelry Accessories. For about six months, I was nervous and I let my inventory sit in the same box it had come in. Around November of that year, our upline challenged us to go live on Facebook every day. I love a good challenge, and I won the prize!

As I continued going live, I really enjoyed being myself and having a great time. I call it "Slinging Bling," because I am my own boss. I get to say whatever I want to say and do whatever I want to do. From time to time, I like to check the data of my views and sales. What I noticed is that people pay attention to me, and I am good at running my business. It has taken me a while to become established as an entrepreneur, but I am here now and I am not going back.

Real Estate

There was a time when my dreams for entrepreneurship had waned, but around 2019 I began to envision owning my own business, again. The desire for more rose up in me and I could not keep still. Takyia was 16 years old at that time, doing high school things. Because she was driving, I was not needed as much. Being that free was new to me; I had to figure out who I wanted to be besides Takyia's mom.

I pondered it, and in February 2020, right before the pandemic started, I took a two-day class on real estate offered by Than Merrill, but of course he was not there.

On the second day of the training staff would pull people out of class to go into the lobby to talk. Their intention was to invite us to join the group, and when I had my meeting, the staff member said, "You will be a great fit for us. All you will need to do is pay us $30,000."

My facial expression had to have said what I was thinking, "What the f--.?"

Without blinking the staff member said, "Do you want to pay the fee using a credit card?"

That was a hard hell naw for me. She said, "You do not have to decide today. Go home and talk it over with your husband."

I returned to the classroom and spoke to two classmates about my conversation with the staff member. A couple of days later we met for lunch to discuss the details of starting our own company. We talked about how to get funding and the steps for moving forward from there. About a week after that, I tried to call one member of the team, but his phone was disconnected. That was a red flag for me. I found out that the other member moved from North Carolina to Virginia, and she had some health issues.

Here is a little tip: don't let other people keep you from doing what you want to do. I had to pursue my dream of real estate on my own. I kept my focus, did not get overwhelmed and thought things through to make my own plan.

I was pumped and excited to tell Tremaine the great news that I was going to become a real estate investor. While driving home from the seminar, God and I had a conversation. I said, "Now how will I explain to him that I want to use my credit cards to pay for this, or that we need to take out a second mortgage on our house?"

By the time I got home from the seminar, the speech for my husband changed to, "I am going to open up my own business." When I told my family, they were excited for me and that night, they helped me pick out a name and everything.

Working During The Pandemic

Setting up an LLC during the pandemic was not hard at all. The Secretary of State forms were filled out online, and I had to send a check for $125. On April 17, 2020, my real estate company, Open Door Home Solutions, LLC., was formed in the middle of the pandemic

I flipped two homes. The first property was easy. That second property was a beast and almost kicked my ass but God made a way for me. Then, the pandemic hit and changed everything. The business was just getting started, but by the time I was ready to hit the pavement all of the banks stopped loaning money. Everyone was at a standstill. I had to utilize my own funds to get the business started.

I found a tax person who talked to me about filing out the tax forms. It is very, very important that you have the assistance of a great tax person. Also, you need to have a business bank account. I set up two accounts when I first started. The first bank was the first to respond to me after the banks began opening back up to in-person visits. The second bank was offering money to open up an account. As the checks were rolling out from my mobile notary business I would put my money to work in my business account.

Establishing business credit, I opened several accounts and paid on time, just as I do with my personal accounts. I have been great at managing our house and my money for a long time. I recognize that with inflation, the cost of everything has risen, but my income has remained the same. It is important to stay on top of your money. When things change, adjust and move forward.

I went to Notary school in December of 2020. I had to pivot into something that would provide a safe income for my family and me. Yes, I had my nursing license, but that was not safe for me or my family during COVID-19. I started doing Mobile Notary work, and it was fun for me because I got to leave my house and go on adventures. I am a people person, and even though the pandemic was not over yet, I was masked up and could keep my family and me safe.

At the moment, I am taking a break from investing in real estate. Tremaine and I are still working on buying our dream house with five bedrooms and three bathrooms on an acre of land.

UNSPOKEN TRAUMA

Around 2017, Grandma Shirlene could no longer stay alone in her house. She spent time between Ma's house and with my Aunt Pat in Virginia. Eventually she moved in full-time with my parents. I would visit them every other weekend and I loved when she would tell us stories. Grandma Shirlene grew up in Windsor, North Carolina. Bertie County is in the country with a lot of land and water surrounding it. To this day they still have a lot of floods.

Grandma Shirlene married William "Luck" Eason and they had seven children: four boys and three girls. Even though my grandparents loved each other, as the Persuaders sing in their song, "There is a thin line between love and hate." Grandma Shirlene and Granddaddy stayed married for over fifty years. They were always nice to each other when we were around, and I never imagined that there was violence in their relationship.

I was surprised to hear that Grandaddy once hit Grandma Shirlene in the head with a hammer. She said, "We were walking down the street, and he saw his mistress with her husband, and he got mad."

Ma said that she never remembered Grandma Shirlene fighting back if things got violent, but that day, Grandma Shirlene must have had enough of Granddaddy's shenanigans. He hit her in the head with a hammer, and she hit him back.

Ma was around 13, and she remembers seeing blood on the front steps when she came home from school. When she went in the house, she saw Grandma Shirlene and Granddaddy on the bed holding rags to their heads. Both of them had blood running down their faces. Ma said, "It tickled me that they had tried to kill each other, but still ended up together."

It was shocking for me to hear that they fought that way. Granddaddy was a deacon in the church and he never let us see the mean side of him. I didn't think he could do anything wrong.

The conversation shifted one day when Grandma Shirlene started talking about how she witnessed inappropriate things when she was a child. Everybody in the room got quiet and there was an uncomfortable silence. Everyone had a "What the hell?" question on their faces. The direction of the conversations turned in that moment.

Ma said, "Well you did not do anything when Gloria came to you."

I asked myself, "Okay, where is this going?" I knew something had happened to my mom's sister, Gloria, but I did not know the whole story.

Grandma Shirlene got quiet for a while. I saw shame fall on her, and she hung her head. It looked like she was searching for the words to explain herself; after what seemed like days, she said, "What was I supposed to do? I was caught between a rock and a hard place. Back then women did not have any power or rights to stand up against men. That was a close family member, and I was taught that what happens in the home stays in the home."

For there is nothing hidden
that will not be disclosed,
and nothing concealed
that will not be known
or brought out into the open.

Luke 8:17

AIN'T NO
SHAME

Hearing my mother and grandmother talk about Aunt Gloria and what Grandma experienced, I gained a better understanding of my Aunt Gloria. I knew that she graduated from W.S. Creecy High School in Rich Square, North Carolina. After graduation she moved to New York City to stay with Grandma Shirlene's sister, Viola Farmer. They lived in Harlem, Brooklyn, and in the Bronx. Aunt Gloria prospered in New York. She worked at the Post Office and the Board of Education as a Supervisor of the School Safety Department.

According to her long-time best friend, Linda Ridley, my auntie was the nicest person on this earth. They never argued since the day that they met when they were 12. Linda's poignant recollection of the day they first met gave me chills. "Gloria saved my life," she recounted, and the weight of her reflection describes how God intertwines our paths with each other.

Linda was at the bus stop with her sister on the morning she met my aunt. She was planning to make sure that her sister got to school, but she was going to run away from home. Their grandmother was raising them and she died suddenly. Their father came to move them to a different county, but Linda did not want to live there.

A new home, a new school, and a sea of unfamiliar faces made Linda unhappy. She said, "And then Gloria walked up to me and asked, 'What's your name?' That one question opened the door to a lifelong friendship. I stayed in Woodland, North Carolina and your family became like my family."

I laughed when Linda said, "Your mom was always trying to tag along with us." My mom said she would always try to keep up with them and they "beat my ass all the time, but I wanted to hang with the older girls." I could relate to that because I did the same thing with my older sister and her friends. Although Aunt Gloria and Linda tried to leave my mom, they were all close.

Gloria went to New York and Linda got married but they stayed connected. After Linda's marriage did not work out, she moved from Florida and reunited with Aunt Gloria in New York. Ma took us to visit Aunt Gloria in the Bronx every Thanksgiving and we got to see Ms. Linda, too.

Being from a small town and visiting New York City was like night and day. Aunt Gloria had transformed into a true New Yorker. She did not take sh-t off of anybody, she was not intimidated by anyone or anything, and she adapted to the big city with ease.

When we arrived in New York, Ma gave each of us $150 to spend on new clothes. She saved her money all year so we could buy ourselves something special. We experienced the thrill of Black Friday shopping before it was popular, and we were able to refresh our wardrobes in the middle of the school year.

Aunt Gloria passed away when I was 16 years old and she was 45. She was prepared for her passing because she had her affairs in order with life insurance in place. She had a policy for Ma, and with her money, she and Daddy bought land and a five-bedroom, two-bathroom house.

Unfortunately, due to her unhealed trauma, Aunt Gloria had turned to drugs for comfort. Although her addiction did not impact our relationship, she was a tormented soul with a lot of shame. I think Aunt Gloria's heart finally gave out from all the running she had been doing. She was running from trauma, disappointment, drug abuse, and everything that comes along with shame.

I thought about Aunt Gloria as I was writing my story. I know some people will not understand how I can be so open or vocal about what I have been through, witnessed, and heard. There is still a stigma about sharing personal testimonies in the black community, but I believe that talking about it helps us to get free. Freedom leads to forgiveness. Forgiveness leads to peace.

I empathize with Grandma Shirlene's choice not to pursue charges against the family member who hurt Aunt Gloria. I did not like her choice because I have always wanted to protect my daughters. Thinking about what Aunt Gloria went through, I wish Ma had told us earlier about the cycles of abuse that were in our family. I realized that she never let us spend the night with anyone at their house because she was keeping us close to her to protect us from sexual abuse.

If I had been in Grandma Shirlene's shoes I probably would have beaten somebody's ass or run that man over with a car. If this had happened to one of my children, there would have been some consequences. I adopted the mother bear protection skills from Ma. I had to know everyone who was in my daughter's lives before they spent the night with friends.

During the conversations with the two female anchors in my life, I realized that it was not just Aunt Gloria who had been abused in my family. My great-great,-grandmother, and a male cousin, had been assaulted. In 2009, I had an inkling that I, too, had been assaulted, but memories flooded my mind when Grandma Shirlene and Ma started talking. I could not ignore them anymore. I had to face my own shame.

These conversations opened my eyes.

I did not know so many people in my family had unspoken trauma. I started to think about the family curse that needs to be broken. Because my family kept all of this information quiet, the cycle continued for generations. The silence about these issues meant that the curse could not be broken.

As my family was beginning to talk about these experiences, we were starting to work through some of the pain and trauma. That helped us get the freedom to move forward individually and collectively. God was exposing the hurt so we could begin to heal. We continued to have these conversations until Grandma Shirlene passed in 2019.

I started a different type of healing journey in 2022 after a car accident. I was hit from behind and went to my primary doctor the next day. Everything seemed to be fine, but my body was hurting. I was already in therapy, but memories of the assault kept coming to me in dreams and visions. I kept trying to push them down but they would not leave me alone. My therapist said, "All of the defense mechanisms you used in the past are not working anymore."

I had to be honest with my therapist about my traumas, that included the sexual violation that I never talked about. She taught me how to move past painful situations using mindful thinking and calming techniques. We were making good headway, but after a few months my insurance would no longer pay her. That made me more vulnerable to negative thoughts. My anxiety was flaring up and my depression was kicking in. I was having a rough time and I had to lean on God.

IT TAKES FAITH

On September 19, 2020, Tremaine decided we
were mountain climbing and repelling. I
usually enjoy hiking and sitting by the
waterfalls. Being in God's presence is peaceful
for me. Tremaine planned everything, which
made me nervous because I am usually the
planner. I said "Okay," and even though I was
so scared, I pressed on anyway. We drove to
Morganton, North Carolina to explore and
people-watch before resting up for the
adventure of Saturday morning.

We went to Pisgah National Forest; its
elevation is as tall as 5,800 feet. I could see
how high the peaks were from the car. We
arrived on time to what we thought was our
destination after driving on the narrow roads,
but it turned out that we were on the wrong
side of the mountain. I had to drive down and
back up the correct side.

When we arrived at the designated meet-
up location, there were no parking spaces. I
found a grassy area and made my own spot so
we could hurry to meet our group. Tremaine
and I headed up the trail, hiking about two
miles to catch the group. I was distracted by

the excitement and I did not realize how much walking we were doing and how high we were.

When we finally saw the group and I had time to catch my breath, I looked at the huge mountain in front of us with a widened gaze. "We are expected to climb that?" I thought to myself. To say I was scared is an understatement.

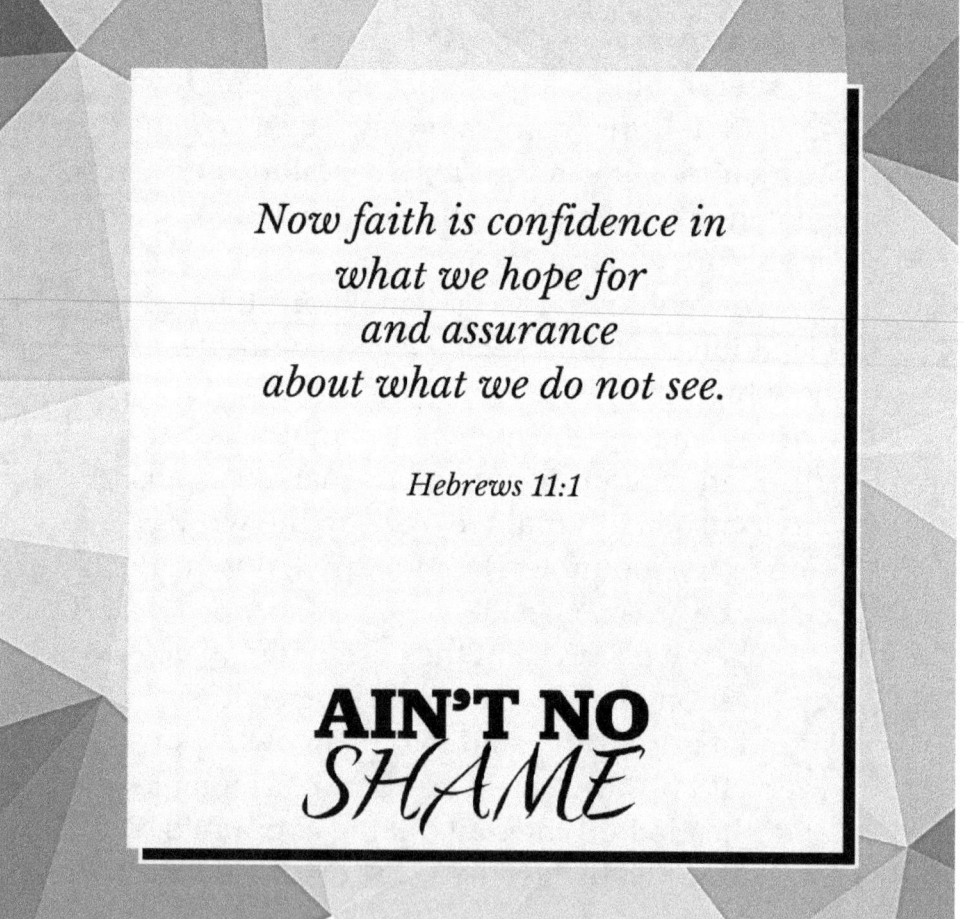

Now faith is confidence in what we hope for and assurance about what we do not see.

Hebrews 11:1

AIN'T NO *SHAME*

The instructor led us so high up the mountain that I could see eagles flying. My nerves and a little bit of anger started to set in. Tremaine didn't explain how big this area, or this mountain would be. I could not believe this was the beginner's class or that I was the only one in the group who had never done anything like this before. We put on our climbing gear and used powder to help with the friction on our hands. I was willing to try climbing the mountain and I jumped right in. As I lifted my body, I would find a part of the mountain for my hands to grip. Everything was going well until halfway up the mountain; I could not get my body to go any further. That was all I had in the tank; my upper body strength was not the best, and I was tired.

After the mountain climb, we went up a little higher. This is where I had already made up in my mind. "Oh, hell naw I am not doing that," I thought to myself. "Nope not a chance!"

I cheered for everyone and took pictures of them. My husband started showing off; he went down like three times, and the group convinced me it was a good idea for me to try it. The instructor was trying to complete the class session, but real talk, I was scared. I told him, "The only way that I am going to repel down this mountain is if you go with me."

Well, he called my bluff. The instructor attached me to him with a carabiner and a rope. I looked like I was his pet on a leash and that was perfectly alright with me. The instructor was below me, waiting for me. "Step back," he says.

I looked back and saw that there was no mountain behind me. I was not okay, ya'll. The only thing back there was air. I tell him, "There is nothing back there to step on." In that moment I had a whole conversation with the Lord, there was maybe a curse word or two said but after some negotiations I finally stepped back. My legs had no idea what to do, and I crashed into the mountain with my whole body. My legs and knees hit the hardest, but I was finally off the cliff. We continued down the mountain, and when we reached the bottom, I was excited and proud of myself. I had tried something new and different; it took me a while to get it together. I got it done, I do not think I will ever repel down the side of a mountain, but I will try climbing again.

As I reflect on my life, I realize that God has had me connected to Him the whole time, like I was connected to my climbing instructor. For that, I am grateful.

YOU CAN OVERCOME SHAME

I have experienced shame as embarrassment, feeling less than, and unworthy. Shame has impacted my life in many ways, and I have, at times allowed it to hold me back, causing moments of anxiety and depression. I have been ashamed to talk about my experiences being verbally abused and allowing other people to control me with their words. When I was feeling ashamed, I allowed others to use me outside of God's purpose. Thank God I have been delivered!

I have committed self-abuse by over-drinking and passing out in clubs. It is hard to admit that I have vomited on myself and had to crawl down a hallway to get to the bathroom. In my mind, I was just trying to catch up on the things I thought I missed out on because I got married so young. The truth is, overindulging on alcohol was my way of trying to forget some of the negative life experiences in my life.

Shame Defined

*a painful feeling of
humiliation or emotion
caused by guilt, or shortcomings*

*distress caused by
the consciousness of wrong behavior.*

~Webster's Dictionary

AIN'T NO
SHAME

No one has it all together. At some point in life we all need help. I turned to God to help me overcome my shame. I have made changes in my life with God's help. First, I cut back on my drinking and I avoid brown liquor. I have seen what too much drinking can do. I have witnessed the damage it can cause on both sides of my family. I do not want my children to see that ever, and I definitely do not want them to see alcoholism within me.

My life is awesome. I am learning to love myself more and more. I am happy, loved, and free. God has been my source and sometimes I must remind myself of this, but I am truly blessed.

I work consistently on myself with God. To maintain my joy I do a few things such as hydrotherapy. I like swimming, taking long showers and going to the beach. Talking to God and writing down my prayers helps me keep shame at bay. For fun I love singing, dancing, drinking Icees, window shopping, and making others laugh. Humor is one of my tools to combat shame. When I feel overwhelmed I talk with my family or pray.

Count It All Joy

As a product of what I have been through, I am passionate, resilient, tenacious and filled with gratitude. In my walk with God, I have learned that through trials and tribulations, He builds our character with His character traits:

- Holiness
- Wisdom
- Truthfulness
- Love
- Goodness
- Faithfulness
- Mercy
- Kindness
- Patience
- Justice and
- Righteousness

In one of his sermons, TD Jakes said, "Let go of your little plan and accept that God's plan is best." Once I heard him say that I immediately began to pray aloud, "I don't want to do anything that is not a benefit to You, Lord." I asked Him to help me embrace the past, accept the present, and move on to the future.

I want to honor God and make Him proud. This book is not just for me. It is for you. Sometimes we need to ask God for forgiveness and seek the truth. Our minds and hearts need to be open and accepting of what He has planned for us.

Do Your Work

Do your work; don't live in shame. What is your vision for yourself? Are you hungry? Are you tired? Are you sick and tired of being tired? Are you tired of living your life in shame? When is enough going to be enough for you to be open and honest with yourself. Take off your mask and live in your truth.

I told you my story. My goal is to help you think positive. Listen to me clearly. I know our world is full of bad stuff, but how I handle it is by praying and giving it to God. He can handle all of these things way better than we can.

I changed my thinking by going to therapy. In therapy, I learned how to love myself more and love my family correctly. And if I am going to keep it real with you, God is the foundation of it all. He will help you do your work to heal from shame.

I have been seeing a therapist for a while. Yes, I know many Black people don't go to therapy. But let me tell you, we should. We walk around upset about sh-t someone said to us back when we were seven years old. That hurt shows up from time to time in other ways.

I used to see a male therapist, and during one session, he told me in air quotes that my problems, "Seem to be lady problems." For a moment I was offended. My eyes got big at that point, and my husband probably would have said something like, "Your nostrils are flaring, Treisha."

My therapist recommended that I speak with a female therapist and it turned out he was right. I had more things in common with the female therapist I found, and she understood where I was coming from. She listened to me and offered tools to help me change my thinking. I really enjoyed that my therapist was intentional about always to include God into our discussions.

Speak positively, and you will get positive back. Try it and see how it works out for you. There are days when I am not on my best behavior, but once I recognize that I am messing up I try my best to adjust my thinking and change my behavior.

It will be hard, it will be frustrating, and you will get angry, but it will all be worth it in the end. Ain't no shame in talking about what you have been through. This is your life and your experiences have made you who you are today. Live in peace. Walk in joy. Embrace faith.

TOOLS FOR OVERCOMING SHAME

SUGGESTED READING

I did not realize that I was an avid reader until I thought about some books I had read that helped me overcome my shame, love my husband more, pray for my children more and learn more about myself. Reading helped me understand areas in my life where I needed to grow spiritually, mentally, and emotionally.

- Capps, Charles. *God's Creative Power for Healing.*
- Chapman, Gary. *The Five Love Languages: The Secret to Love the Lasts*
- Omartian, Stormie. *The Power of a Praying Wife.*
- Omartian, Stormie. *The Power of Praying for Your Adult Children.*
- Palau, Luis. *God At The Center: Habits For Spiritual Growth.*
- Robinson, Nefateria F. *How to ACT: Activate Faith, Commit to a Plan, Take Action That Will Change Your Life.*
- Word Ministries. *Prayers that Avail Much.*

MEDITATION SCRIPTURES

Cast all your cares on the Lord.
I Peter 5:7

Favor is deceitful and beauty is vain but a woman that fears the Lord she shall be praised.
Proverbs 31:30

For the Scripture says, 'Whoever believes in Him will not be put to shame.
Romans 10:11

If we confess our sins, He is faithful and just to forgive us our sins and to cleanse us from all unrighteousness.
1 John 1:9

Give thanks to the God of heaven.
His love endures forever.
Psalm 136:26 (NIV)

Do not be anxious about anything, but in every situation, by prayer and petition, with thanksgiving, present your requests to God.
Philippians 4:6 (NIV)

Now faith is confidence in what we hope for and assurance about what we do not see.
Hebrews 11:1 (NIV)

Commit thy way unto the Lord;
trust also in him; and he shall bring it to pass.
Psalm 37:5

Trust in the Lord with all thine heart; and lean not
unto thine own understanding.
In all thy ways acknowledge him,
and he shall direct thy paths.
Proverbs 3:5-6

SOME OF MY FAVORITE SONGS

- "Feel Alright" Erica Campbell
- "Go Get It" Mary Mary
- "Goodness of God" CeCe Winans
- "Hang On" GEI
- "He's Able" Darwin Hobbs & Dietrich Haddon
- "Hold On" Sounds of Blackness
- "I Rely" Semaje
- "In spite of Me" Tasha Cobbs-Leonard
- "It's Gone Be Alright" Tye Tribbett
- "Jireh" Maverick City Music
- "Manifestation" Jakalyn Carr
- "Open Door Season" Deitrick Haddon
- "Optimistic" Sounds of Blackness
- "The Battle" Yolanda Adams
- "This Week" Anthony Brown and Group Therapy
- "When I Pray" Doe
- "Miracles" Kierra Sheard
- "Thank You Lord" Mary Mary
- "You Know my Name" Tasha Cobbs Leonard
- "I Just Wanna Praise You" Maurette Brown Clark

READERS GUIDE QUESTIONS

Aint No Shame talks about some delicate subjects. This book is for people who have been through something that caused them to feel ashamed, and they have a hard time overcoming it. I will be the voice that will not keep silent to help you break free from shame.

The following questions are conversation starters that will help you as an individual, or your group reflect and gather gems to overcome shame and lean on God.

What can you sacrifice in your life to overcome shame?

_____
_____
_____
_____
_____
_____
_____
_____
_____

***

Is therapy an option for you? Why or why not?

_____
_____
_____
_____
_____
_____
_____
_____
_____
_____
_____
_____

Who is in your circle?

_____

_____

_____

_____

_____

_____

_____

_____

***

What are you going to do about your
happiness?

_____

_____

_____

_____

_____

_____

_____

_____

_____

_____

_____

How do you let your light shine?

_____

_____

_____

_____

_____

_____

_____

_____

_____

_____

***

Talk about moments of shame that you have
experienced and how you overcame them.

_____

_____

_____

_____

_____

_____

_____

_____

_____

_____

_____

_____

_____

_____

_____

What do you say to yourself about yourself?

_____

_____

_____

_____

_____

_____

_____

_____

_____

_____

_____

_____

***

Describe a pivotal moment when you had to
overcome shame.

_____

_____

_____

_____

_____

_____

_____

_____

What is God's passion for you?

_____

_____

_____

_____

_____

_____

_____

_____

_____

_____

_____

_____

**

How can you be more aligned with God?

_____

_____

_____

_____

_____

_____

_____

_____

_____

_____

What is your vision for your life?

_____

_____

_____

_____

_____

_____

_____

_____

_____

_____

_____

***

How do you plan to get there?

_____

_____

_____

_____

_____

_____

_____

_____

What are some of your favorite scriptures that helped you overcome shame?

_____
_____
_____
_____
_____
_____
_____
_____
_____
_____
_____
_____
_____
_____
_____
_____
_____
_____
_____
_____
_____
_____
_____

Share your favorite quotes from the book.

_____
_____
_____
_____
_____
_____
_____
_____
_____
_____
_____
_____
_____
_____
_____
_____
_____
_____
_____
_____
_____
_____
_____
_____

Create a playlist to help someone overcome shame and turn to God.

_____

_____

_____

_____

_____

_____

_____

_____

_____

_____

_____

_____

_____

_____

_____

_____

_____

_____

_____

_____

_____

_____

_____

*Instead of your shame
you will receive
a double portion,
and instead of disgrace
you will rejoice in your
inheritance.*

Isaiah 61:7 (NIV)

AIN'T NO
SHAME

ABOUT THE AUTHOR

The joy of the Lord is Treisha Parker-Combo's strength. She strives to be a living example of God's grace. With her kind and gentle demeanor, she strives to share God's love with others. "Life has taught me well," she says, "I could complain but it wouldn't change anything."

A woman of many talents, Treisha is an LPN, a financial services educator, a real estate investor, an entrepreneur, and a digital Creator. Twice a week, wearing her signature sunglasses and bright smile, she spreads positive messages of hope through social media livestreams. Her message is simple, she wants people to experience joy and live in peace.

Ms. Parker-Combo resides in Smithfield, North Carolina. She is a wife, a mother, a daughter, and a friend to many. *Ain't No Shame* is Treisha's first book.

www.ingramcontent.com/pod-product-compliance
Lightning Source LLC
Chambersburg PA
CBHW060328130626
46553CB00003B/947